Bible Activities
FOR
Class & Home

Reproducible Activities For Grades 1 & 2

Publisher..Art Miley

Managing Editor...Carol Rogers

Editor and Compiler...Mark Rasche

Production Assistant..Chris D. Neynaber

Illustrators...Various

Cover Designer...Court Patton

Proofreader..Heather Swindle

Copyright 1996 ● Second Printing
Rainbow Books ● P.O. Box 261129 ● San Diego, CA 9219

D0989287

RB36303
ISBN 1-885358-091

Bible Activities FOR Class & Home

Reproducible Activities For Grades 1 & 2

HOW TO USE THIS BOOK

The purpose of these reproducible activities is to teach young children what it means to trust and love God, make responsible choices, and to live their lives according to God's principles in practical ways.

The activities and projects are designed to be used in the classroom or home under the direction of a teacher, leader or parent. They are ideal for Sunday school, Bible clubs, Christian schools and home schooling. The Bible activities may be done in class and the family projects taken home. **We encourage the reproduction of activity pages for each child or student.** Remember to photocopy the back side of pages that require cutting or pasting.

This publication brings new fun and variety to Bible learning and is intended to supplement and reinforce God's Word. The activities are created especially for the interests and learning abilities of children between first and second grades.

This book contains 58 perforated activity sheets, each including:

> **BIBLE MEMORY VERSE** — taken from both the KING JAMES VERSION (KJV) and the NEW INTERNATIONAL VERSION (NIV).

> **BIBLE ACTIVITY** — an enjoyable activity related to the Bible verse.

> **FAMILY PROJECT** — an opportunity for the whole family to get involved.

For a quick and convenient way to find just the right activity for your lesson, see the Memory Verse Index on page five.

Our hope is that this book will help the Bible come alive for young children. Have fun teaching the boys and girls God's Word!

TABLE OF CONTENTS

MEMORY VERSE INDEX

The Good Shepherd

 ## Memory Verse

John 10:11 — *"I am the Good Shepherd: the Good Shepherd giveth His life for the sheep."* (KJV)

"I am the Good Shepherd. The Good Shepherd lays down His life for the sheep." (NIV)

 ## Bible Activity

FIND THE SHEEP

Can you help the shepherd find the sheep? There are more than eight sheep hidden in this picture. Color the sheep as you find them.

Answer: There are 10 sheep

 ## Family Project

MAKE A SHEEP MOBILE

Find a branch outside and pretend that it is a shepherd's staff. From the branch hang one construction paper sheep for every member of your family. Write each person's name on a sheep. As you look at your sheep mobile remember that the Lord is your Shepherd.

Jesus Is with Me

 Memory Verse

Hebrews 13:5 — *"He hath said, I will never leave thee, nor forsake thee."* (KJV)

"God has said, 'Never will I leave you; never will I forsake you.'" (NIV)

 Bible Activity

WHERE IS JESUS?

In the box below you will find something that reminds us of Jesus. Color each space with a dot in it to find the hidden picture. Then turn the page on its side. What did you find?

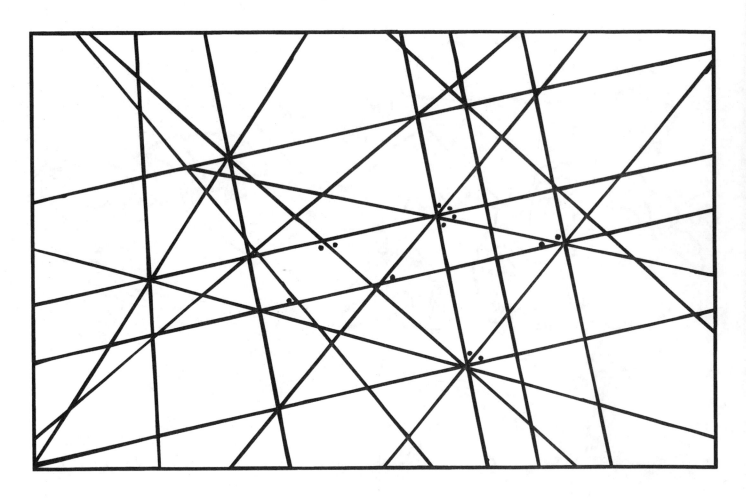

Answer: A cross

 Family Project

A REMINDER ON YOUR MIRROR

Ask your parents to take you to an airport to watch the planes take off and land; or go to a lake and watch the boats. Say your memory verse to your parents. Print the verse on an index card and tape it to a mirror in your home. When you look into the mirror, remember that Jesus is with you.

God Is with You

 Memory Verse

Joshua 1:9 — *"The LORD thy God is with thee whithersoever thou goest."* (KJV)

"The LORD your God will be with you wherever you go." (NIV)

 Bible Activity

LET'S GO FISHING

Cut out the fish, glue a small paper clip to the back of each fish, put the fish in a jar or big bowl, tie string to the end of a stick or a pencil, glue a small magnet to the end of the string, and see how many fish you can catch. Good fishing!

 Family Project

PLAN A PICNIC

Ask your mom and dad to help you plan a family picnic. Decide what food you'll take and where you'll go. Choose a Bible verse to read to the family after you eat. Today's memory verse would be a good verse to read. Choose friends to go along with you on the picnic. Write invitations to them. Have a great picnic!

Jesus Is Loving

 ## Memory Verse

I John 3:1 — *"Behold, what manner of love the Father hath bestowed upon us."* (KJV)

"How great is the love the Father has lavished on us." (NIV)

 ## Bible Activity

WHAT GREAT LOVE
Color the picture according to the numbers:
COLOR: 1 — Red, 2 — Blue, 3 — Green, 4 — Yellow, 5 — Brown.

 ## Family Project

MAKE A BOOKMARK

With a parent's permission, cut a small bookmark from an old manila folder or a sheet of poster board. Measure a 2 x 6-inch space on the folder. Draw a cross at the top of the bookmark. Color the cross red. Print "JESUS LOVES ME" below the cross. Use the bookmark in your Bible.

God Made Everything

 Memory Verse

Psalm 74:17 — *"Thou hast made summer and winter."* (KJV)

"You made both summer and winter." (NIV)

 Bible Activity

MAKE A SNOWFLAKE

God makes the snowflakes. Every snowflake has six sides, but no two are alike. Make a snowflake. Cut out the square. Fold up dotted lines (1), (2), and (3). Turn over and cut line (4). Cut out the four triangles. Unfold your six-sided snowflake.

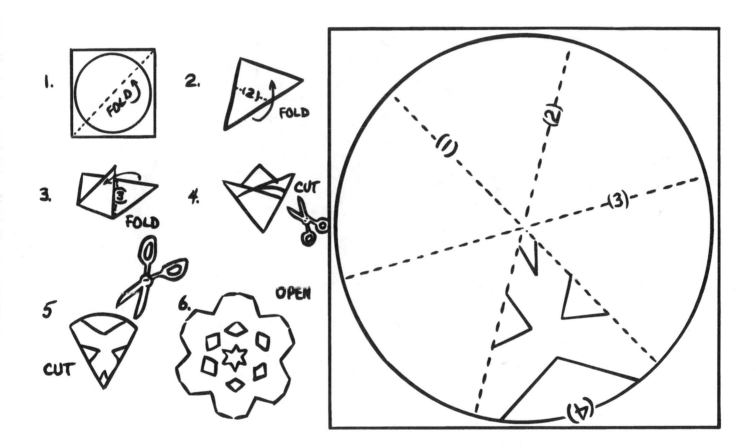

 Family Project

TAKE A WALK

Take a walk with your parent. Do you live where it snows? Are the trees bare? Or are flowers blooming? Is the sky cloudy? Or is the sun shining? Discuss the winter season with your parent. Talk about what you can do in the winter that you can't do any other time (make a snowman, play winter games). Thank God for winter.

God Blesses Me

 Memory Verse

Ephesians 1:3 — *"God...hath blessed us with all spiritual blessings...in Christ."* (KJV)

"God...has blessed us...with every spiritual blessing in Christ." (NIV)

 Bible Activity

TRUE RICHES
To discover where true spiritual riches are found, go around the coin. Print every capital letter in the blank spaces below.

START HERE →

Answer: Heaven

 Family Project

MAKE A LIST OF YOUR BLESSINGS
Discuss with your parent some of the good things God has given you (such as your family, your church, your friends, a home in heaven, etc.). Write them on a sheet of paper. Then tape the paper to your bathroom mirror. Help everyone remember to thank God for His blessings.

He Delivers Me

 Memory Verse

Daniel 6:16 — *"Thy God Whom thou servest continually, He will deliver thee."* (KJV)

"May your God, Whom you serve continually, rescue you!" (NIV)

 Bible Activity

DANIEL'S PRAYER

In the corner of each picture is a secret word. Match it to the blank with that number and write it in the blank. When you are finished writing the words, read the promise about God.

Answer: He careth for you.

 Family Project

MAKE A PAINTING

Using colored chalk, draw a picture of Daniel and a lion on white paper. With a slightly dampened sponge, lightly pat the picture and you will create a velvet-like painting. Tape a string to the top ends of the paper so you can hang it in your room.

Trust the Lord

Memory Verse

Isaiah 26:4 — *"Trust ye in the LORD for ever: for in the LORD JEHOVAH is everlasting strength."* (KJV)

"Trust in the LORD forever, for the LORD, the LORD, is the Rock eternal." (NIV)

Bible Activity

BLONDIN'S ADVENTURE

A man named Blondin was a tight-wire artist, and in 1860 he had faith that he would be able to push a wheelbarrow across a wire that was strung 160 feet above Niagara Falls. He did. Find the hidden word F—A—I—T—H. Circle the letters you find.

Family Project

MAKE A MEMORY VERSE PUZZLE

Glue a sheet of construction paper to cardboard cut from an old cardboard box. The back of a cereal box works well. Print on it, "TRUST YE IN THE LORD FOREVER"— Isaiah 26:4. Ask an adult to cut the puzzle into six pieces. Put the puzzle back together to review your memory verse.

Jesus in My Heart

 ## Memory Verse

John 3:16 — *"For God so loved the world, that He gave His only begotten Son, that whosoever believeth in Him should not perish, but have everlasting life."* (KJV)

"For God so loved the world that He gave His one and only Son, that whoever believes in Him shall not perish but have eternal life." (NIV)

 ## Bible Activity

A CLOSER LOOK

This is an optical illusion. That means your eyes see something that is not really happening. Looking at the space between Jesus and the heart, bring the paper closer to your eyes, and when the paper is almost on your nose, Jesus will be in the heart.

 ## Family Project

MAKE A GOOD FRIEND

Show God's love to someone who is new at school. Invite this person to sit with you and your friends during lunch. Ask if he or she would visit your church. Invite this person to come over to your house to play.

Faith in Jesus

Memory Verse

Ephesians 2:8-9 — *"By grace are ye saved through faith...it is the gift of God: not of works."* (KJV)

"By grace you have been saved, through faith...it is the gift of God — not by works." (NIV)

Bible Activity

FIND THE WAY

Don't get sidetracked by some other things! See if you can find the way that goes straight to heaven. Draw a line from the boy that goes straight to heaven.

Family Project

MAKE A HEART CARD

Let's make a Forgiven Heart card. Draw a picture of Jesus. Cut a heart out of red construction paper (an adult can help). Have an adult cut a door in the center of the heart so the picture of Jesus, taped to the back, shows through it. Print the words to Ephesians 2:8-9 on the front of the card.

Bible Activities for Class and Home, Grades 1 and 2

Whiter than Snow

 ## Memory Verse

Psalm 51:7 — *"Wash me, and I shall be whiter than snow."* (KJV)

"Wash me, and I will be whiter than snow." (NIV)

 ## Bible Activity

COLOR BY NUMBER
Color the spaces below as follows: 1-brown, 2-red, and 3-blue. You will discover a hidden picture.

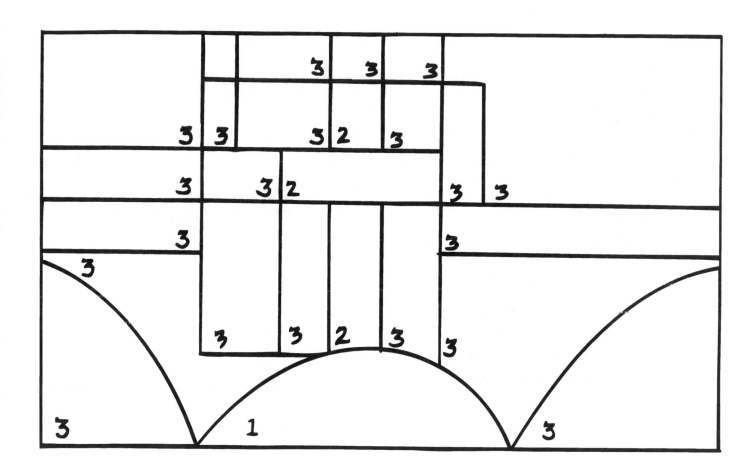

Answer: The picture is a cross on a hill.

 ## Family Project

A HEART FOR YOUR ROOM

On a piece of white construction paper, draw the outline of a large heart. Cut it out. Then write the memory verse on it. Ask a parent to help you put a loop of yarn through the top of the heart. Hang it in your bedroom to remind you of the verse.

Trust in God Only

 ## Memory Verse

Psalm 118:9 — *"It is better to trust in the LORD than to put confidence in princes."* (KJV)

"It is better to take refuge in the LORD than to trust in princes." (NIV)

 ## Bible Activity

PAUL AND BARNABAS MAZE
Paul and Barnabas healed a lame man. The crowd wanted to worship Paul and Barnabas. Some angry people tried to stone Paul. Help Paul and Barnabas get from Lystra to the next city they fled to after Paul was stoned by a mob of people.

LYSTRA

 ## Family Project

MAKE A WRIST BAND

Print "TRUST GOD" on an 8 x 1-inch band of construction paper. (Have an adult or older brother or sister help you measure for the band, then cut it out.) Tape the paper band around your wrist as a reminder to trust God through the day. If anyone asks what you are wearing, tell this person that it reminds you to trust God.

Share the News

 ## Memory Verse

Romans 10:9 — *"If thou shalt confess with thy mouth the Lord Jesus, and shalt believe in thine heart that God hath raised Him from the dead, thou shalt be saved."* (KJV)

"If you confess with your mouth, 'Jesus is Lord', and believe in your heart that God raised Him from the dead, you will be saved." (NIV)

 ## Bible Activity

WAYS TO SHARE

There are many ways to share the Good News about Jesus. One way is to talk about it. Circle the pictures below that show other ways we can share Good News about Jesus.

Answer: Circle 1, 3, 4, 5.

 ## Family Project

MAKE A GOOD NEWS SIGN

You can make a sign to share the Good News of Jesus. Make a sign that says, "ASK ME ABOUT JESUS" from a circle of construction paper. Tape a yarn loop on the back to hang it up. Big signs can hang on doorknobs. Little signs can hang on buttons. Wear one to school. Make extras to give away. Be ready to tell more about Jesus if someone asks.

Strong Faith

Memory Verse

Ephesians 6:10 — *"Be strong in the Lord, and in the power of His might."* (KJV)

"Be strong in the Lord and in His mighty power." (NIV)

Bible Activity

WHAT MAKES US STRONG?

Do you know what you need to be strong against Satan? Find out by connecting the dots. If you're not sure what it is, Ephesians 6:16 will tell you. But first unscramble the following letters and print them on the proper blanks on the cross: TAFIH

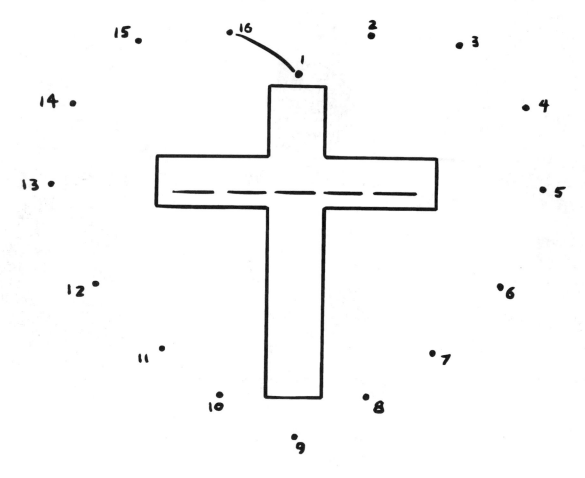

Answer: Faith

Family Project

MAKE SOME FUN-TIME PUTTY

Make some Fun-time Putty. Ask a parent to help you. Mix together in a bowl 1 tablespoon of starch and 2 tablespoons of white glue. Let the mixture set for five minutes. Then have fun making a paperweight with the putty. Use a cookie cutter design of your choice. With a nail, print "FAITH" on the paperweight.

Stand Firm

 ## Memory Verse

Psalm 31:6 — *"I trust in the LORD."*
(KJV & NIV)

 ## Bible Activity

WHAT SHOULD YOU TRUST?
Cross out the things a Christian should not trust. Draw a circle around what a Christian should trust.

HORSESHOE

WISHING WELL

LUCKY STAR

RABBIT'S FOOT

FOUR-LEAF CLOVER

JESUS

Answer: Cross out everything but Jesus, Who should be circled.

 ## Family Project

MAKE A PLACE MAT

With your parent's help (or on your own), print "TRUST IN THE LORD" on a sheet of large white paper. Draw and color flowers or ask a parent to help you press flowers on your place mat. Clear adhesive paper can be placed over the place mat. As you use your place mat, remember to trust in the Lord.

Happy in Jesus

 ## Memory Verse

Proverbs 16:20 — *"Whoso trusteth in the LORD, happy is he."* (KJV)

"Blessed is he who trusts in the LORD." (NIV)

 ## Bible Activity

HIDDEN PICTURE
Count the happy faces you find in this scene. Remember that only Jesus brings true happiness. Then count the sad faces in the picture. How many are happy? How many are sad?

Answers: 13 happy, 13 sad.

 ## Family Project

MAKE A HAPPY SCENE

Ask your parent to cut out one side of an empty pint-sized milk carton. Glue construction paper on the sides of the carton. Draw a happy scene on white paper and color it. Then glue it to the inside of the carton. Print the memory verse on white paper and glue it to the top of the carton.

Love the Lord

 ## Memory Verse

Mark 12:30 — *"And thou shalt love the Lord thy God with all thy heart, and with all thy soul, and with all thy mind, and with all thy strength."* (KJV)

"Love the Lord your God with all your heart and with all your soul and with all your mind and with all your strength." (NIV)

 ## Bible Activity

HEARTS FOR THE LORD

On each heart below, print a way in which you can show love for the Lord. Cut out the hearts. At suppertime, give each member of your family a glass of water decorated with a heart-message taped to it. (If more hearts are needed, use these as a pattern to make others.)

 ## Family Project

A HEART FOR YOUR REFRIGERATOR

Trace around one of the hearts used on this activity page. Then cut out a heart from red construction paper. Print "Love the Lord your God with all your heart and with all your soul and with all your mind and with all your strength." — Mark 12:30 (NIV) on your heart. Attach the heart to the door of your refrigerator with a refrigerator magnet.

Love Others

Memory Verse

Romans 13:9 — *"Thou shalt not kill, Thou shalt not steal, Thou shalt not bear false witness, Thou shalt not covet...Thou shalt love thy neighbour as thyself."* (KJV)

"'Do not murder','Do not steal,' 'Do not covet,'...'Love your neighbor as yourself.'" (NIV)

Bible Activity

COLOR THE PICTURES
Color the pictures that show love for others. Circle the number of the pictures that show ways you can show love to someone.

Answer: Color 1, 2, and 6.

Family Project

HELP YOUR NEIGHBOR

Ask your parents to help you buy some food for a homeless family. Make sure the food is in cans or boxes and is not perishable (fresh food that has to be used up soon or it will go bad). Choose some good clothes of yours that are too little for you. Take these things to a family who needs them.

Good Habits

 ## Memory Verse

I Samuel 3:9 — *"Speak, LORD; for Thy servant heareth."* (KJV)

"Speak, LORD, for Your servant is listening." (NIV)

 ## Bible Activity

GOOD HABITS — BAD HABITS
What are good habits and what are bad habits? Circle the picture if it shows a good habit. Draw a cross through the picture if it shows a bad habit.

1

2

3

WOW

4

5

6

BIBLE

Answers: Circle 1, 2, 4 & 6; Cross out 3 & 5

 ## Family Project

MAKE A GOOD HABIT CHART

Ask your parents to help you list on a chart good habits you should do daily and bad habits you should not do. Each time you do a good habit, draw a smiling face beside it. Draw a frowning face beside any bad habit you do. Ask Jesus to help you have lots of smiling faces on your chart.

Seek Jesus

 ## Memory Verse

Matthew 6:33 — *"Seek ye first the kingdom of God, and His righteousness."* (KJV)

"Seek first His kingdom and His righteousness." (NIV)

 ## Bible Activity

THE WAY TO JESUS
Find the way to Jesus. Avoid the wrong way. Draw a line from the child to Jesus without crossing any lines.

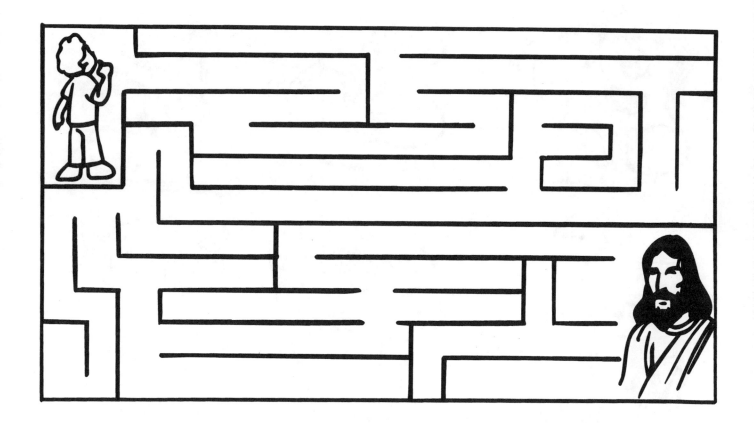

 ## Family Project

DRAW PUPPETS

Draw puppet faces on two paper plates, one smiling and one frowning. Glue a long stick to each. Print "JESUS FIRST" on a card to glue under the happy face. Print "ME FIRST" on a card to glue under the frowning face. Put the puppets in your room to remind you to put Jesus first to be happy.

Think First

Memory Verse

Proverbs 14:15 — *"The simple believeth every word: but the prudent man looketh well to his going."* (KJV)

"A simple man believes anything, but a prudent man gives thought to his steps." (NIV)

Bible Activity

WHAT SHOULD HE HAVE SAID?

What should the prophet of God have said when an old false prophet told him to go home with him because an angel had said it would be okay? Connect the dots and you will find out. This is the same word you should say if a stranger stops you.

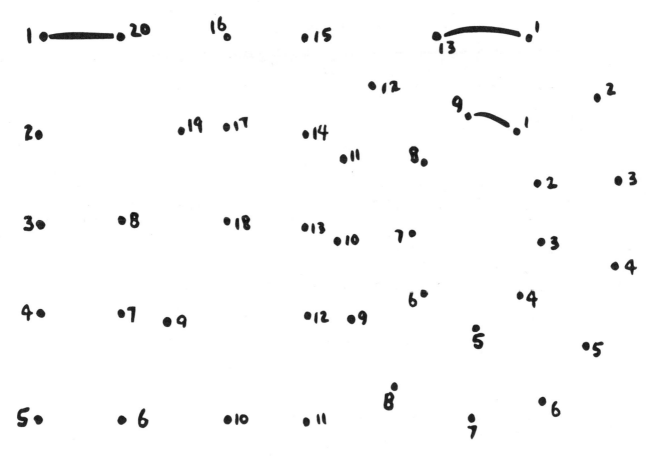

Answer: No

Family Project

INVISIBLE MEMORY VERSE

Using a Q-tip dipped in lemon juice, write your memory verse in invisible ink on a piece of white paper. Give it to a friend. Tell him or her to heat the paper by holding it close to a light bulb. The heat will bring out the words so he or she will be able to read it.

Work with Your Heart

 ## Memory Verse

Colossians 3:23 — *"Whatsoever ye do, do it heartily, as to the Lord."* (KJV)

"Whatever you do, work at it with all your heart, as working for the Lord." (NIV)

 ## Bible Activity

HELP WANTED!

Fill in your name, the date you will help by doing a job for Mom or Dad, and the job you will do. After you finish the job, ask your Mom or Dad to sign your Helper Certificate.

Helper Certificate

_____
(your name)

pleased Jesus by being a helper on

_____
(date)

This person did this job:

_____

Signed: _____
(parent)

 ## Family Project

MAKE A HELP CHART

Have a parent or older brother or sister help you to make a chart with seven squares, with one square for each day of the week. Title the chart "MY HELPING CHART." Every day of this week that you do a helping job for a parent, attach a gold gummed star to the square. See if you can score seven stars!

Grow in God's Word

 Memory Verse

I Peter 2:2 — *"As newborn babes, desire the sincere milk of the Word, that ye may grow thereby."* (KJV)

"Like newborn babies, crave pure spiritual milk, so that by it you may grow up in your salvation." (NIV)

 Bible Activity

GROWING UP
What did these living things look like when they were young? Put the number of the picture in the box beside the word.

a. Man ☐

b. Flower ☐

c. Woman ☐

d. Frog ☐

e. Bird ☐

f. Butterfly ☐

5.

4.

2.

6.

1.

3.

FLOWER SEEDS

Answers: a-4, b-3, c-5, d-1, e-6, f-2

 Family Project

MAKE A GROWING CALENDAR

Find a calendar with big spaces or draw seven squares on a paper, heading them with the days of the week from Sunday to Saturday. Draw a happy face on the square for each day this week that you eat everything on your plate at each meal.

Growing in Jesus

 ## Memory Verse

Jeremiah 15:16 — *"Thy Word was unto me the joy and rejoicing of mine heart."* (KJV)

"Your Words...were my joy and my heart's delight." (NIV)

 ## Bible Activity

FOOD TO GROW WITH

Circle the foods which will help you grow as a Christian. Color the foods which will help your body grow.

Answers: Circle the children reading a Bible and praying; color all the rest of the food.

 ## Family Project

HAVE A PICNIC BREAKFAST

Suggest to your parents that you have a picnic breakfast in your yard or at a nearby park. At the picnic, ask your parents to tell you about the breakfast Jesus had with His disciples. After you return home, review today's Bible memory verse.

Follow the Lord

 ## Memory Verse

Psalm 111:10 — *"The fear of the LORD is the beginning of wisdom: a good understanding have all they that do His commandments."* (KJV)

"The fear of the LORD is the beginning of wisdom; all who follow His precepts have good understanding." (NIV)

 ## Bible Activity

WHO'S WISE
What do YOU need to be wise? Each owl has an answer. Cross out the owls that don't help you become wise. Color the other owls gold and color the tree brown and the leaves and grass green.

Answers: Cross out the owls of good looks and money. Color the rest.

 ## Family Project

MAKE A CENTERPIECE MAT

Make a centerpiece mat for your dinner table. Print "THE FEAR OF THE LORD IS THE BEGINNING OF WISDOM" in the middle of a sheet of construction paper. Make a border of leaves and flowers along the edges of the paper. Have an adult place a sheet of clear adhesive paper on top. Another sheet of adhesive paper can be placed on the bottom.

Listen to Jesus

 ## Memory Verse

Matthew 7:24 — *"Whosoever heareth these sayings of Mine, and doeth them, I will liken him unto a wise man, which built his house upon a rock."* (KJV)

"Everyone who hears these words of Mine and puts them into practice is like a wise man who built his house on the rock." (NIV)

 ## Bible Activity

SPECIAL MESSAGE

Cut out the four puzzle pieces on the broken lines and put them together to form a picture that will help you remember today's memory verse.

Answers: To hear Jesus' teachings and obey them is to build your life on Jesus.

 ## Family Project

CHECK YOUR HOUSE

Ask your parents to show you the foundation of your house. Maybe they can take you to see a house that's being built. Tell them Jesus' story of the two builders and recite your memory verse.

Thank the Lord

 Memory Verse

Colossians 3:17 — *"Do all in the name of the Lord Jesus, giving thanks to God and the Father by Him."* (KJV)

"Do it all in the name of the Lord Jesus, giving thanks to God the Father through Him." (NIV)

 Bible Activity

GIVING THANKS
In the space beside the words below, write the number of the picture which illustrates that word.

I AM THANKFUL FOR:

☐ FAMILY

☐ HOME

☐ TOYS

☐ CLOTHES

☐ FOOD

☐ SUNSHINE

☐ FLOWERS

☐ WATER

1. 5. 6. 2. 7. 3. 8. 4.

Answers: 3-family, 1-home, 4-toys, 7-clothes, 8-food, 2-sunshine, 6-flowers, 5-water

 Family Project

MAKE A THANKSGIVING PLACE MAT

What are you thankful for? Decorate a large sheet of construction paper with drawings or pictures cut from magazines of things you are thankful for. Print "THANKS BE TO GOD" on the paper. Ask a parent to cover the paper with clear adhesive paper. Now you have a Thanksgiving place mat!

Pray to the Lord

 ## Memory Verse

Acts 22:10 — *"What shall I do, Lord?"*
(KJV & NIV)

 ## Bible Activity

TALKING TO GOD

When we pray, we talk to God. We can talk to God about anything, anytime. In the pictures below, if it shows something we can talk to God about, print "YES" in the small box. Print "NO" if the picture shows something we can't talk to God about.

Answers: YES in all your boxes. We can talk to God about anything!

 ## Family Project

PRAYING HANDS

Trace around both of your hands, with your fingers apart, on a sheet of construction paper. Cut out your hand tracing. Paste the hands together with one hand slightly underneath the other so that you can see that there are two hands. On both sides print, "I WILL PRAY TO THE LORD."

Go to Church

 ## Memory Verse

Psalm 122:1 — *"I was glad when they said unto me, Let us go into the house of the LORD."* (KJV)

"I rejoiced with those who said to me, 'Let us go to the house of the LORD.'" (NIV)

 ## Bible Activity

MATCH THE WORDS
Match the blanks in the statements to the pictures at the right, selecting the correct picture-word to fill each blank. After you have filled in each statement, you have five reasons why we go to church.

Why go to church:

1. To _____

2. To _____

3. To learn stories from
   the _____

4. To _____

5. To help _____
   know God

Answers: 1. worship; 2. pray; 3. Bible; 4. sing; 5. others

 ## Family Project

MAKE A MOBILE

You and your mom or dad can cut three pieces of paper and make a mobile. Print the memory verse on one piece. Draw a picture of your church and a picture of your family on the other pieces. Tape them on a long piece of yarn. Hang your mobile where you can see it every day and be reminded to look forward to going to your church.

Bible Activities for Class and Home, Grades 1 and 2

Talk to God

Haggai 1:7 — *"Thus saith the LORD of hosts; Consider your ways."* (KJV)

"This is what the LORD Almighty says; 'Give careful thought to your ways.'" (NIV)

 Bible Activity

COLOR THE PICTURE
Discover how you can give careful thought to your ways. Use these colors:
All spaces with 1 are red. All spaces with 2 are blue. All spaces with 3 are yellow. All spaces with 4 are green.

Answer: You can talk to God in prayer.

 Family Project

MAKE AN OFFERING CUP FOR GOD

You and your mom or dad can make a bank out of a small yogurt container. Cut a slit in the lid; cover the container with foil. The next two weeks, put the money you would spend for treats in your bank. Give your bank to a special offering at your church.

Hear the Lord

 ## Memory Verse

Matthew 11:15 — *"He that hath ears to hear, let him hear."* (KJV)

"He who has ears, let him hear." (NIV)

 ## Bible Activity

USE YOUR EARS

Cut out the word blocks and use the numbers to paste them in the correct places below. Then read the Bible verse.

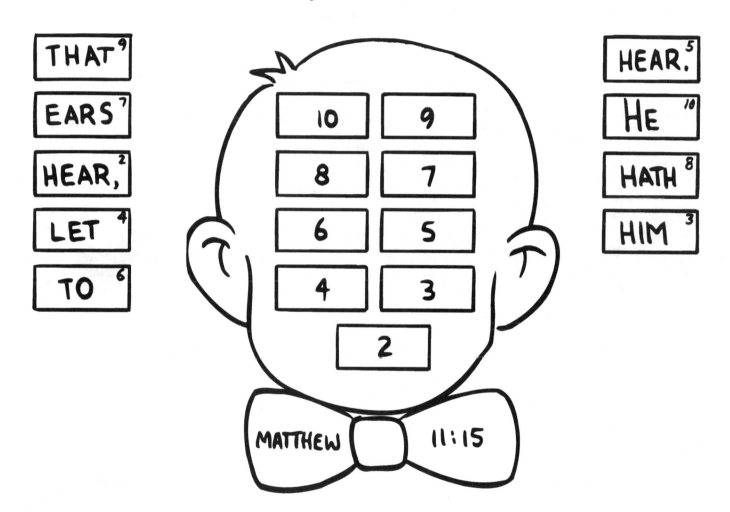

THAT⁹ EARS⁷ HEAR,² LET⁴ TO⁶

HEAR.⁵ HE¹⁰ HATH⁸ HIM³

MATTHEW 11:15

Answer: He that hath ears to hear, let him hear.

 ## Family Project

MAKE A CROSS

Cut a cross from cardboard, measuring 6 inches for the stake and 3 inches for the cross-arm. Punch a hole at the top and attach a loop of yarn. On one side, print "HE THAT HATH EARS TO HEAR, LET HIM HEAR." On the other side, glue small seashells, covering the cross completely. Hang the seashell cross on a wall in your room at home.

Pray for Others

 Memory Verse

Matthew 6:9 — *"After this manner therefore pray ye: Our Father which art in heaven, Hallowed be Thy name."* (KJV)

"This, then, is how you should pray: Our Father in heaven, hallowed be Your name." (NIV)

 Bible Activity

FINISH THE PRAYERS

Here are some prayers you can complete. You can use them to help you pray this week. (Note: When you ask God to do good things for a person you are asking Him to "bless" that person.)

1. Dear heavenly Father, help me to _____ today. I ask this in Jesus' name. Amen.

2. Dear God, please do good things for my family today and take care of them. I ask this in Jesus' name. Amen.

Print the names of everybody in your family here:

_____

_____

_____

_____

_____

 Family Project

MAKE A PAPER-PLATE PICTURE

Glue a Christmas-card picture of Baby Jesus to the center of a plain paper plate. Print "SON OF GOD" above the card and "SAVIOR" below it. Tape a 3-inch loop of yarn to the top back of the plate for hanging. Glue a red bow at the bottom of the plate. Hang the paper-plate picture in your room.

God Hears Our Prayers

 ## Memory Verse

Psalm 6:9 — *"The LORD hath heard my supplication; the LORD will receive my prayer."* (KJV)

"The LORD has heard my cry for mercy; the LORD accepts my prayer." (NIV)

 ## Bible Activity

A SECRET MESSAGE

Print the first letter of each picture in the space below it. For the arrow picture, print the first letter where the arrow points (up or down). For the egg picture, print the first letter of its yellow center. The flower is a rose. Discover an important message!

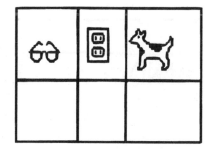

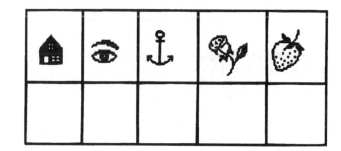

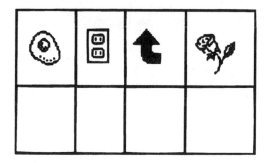

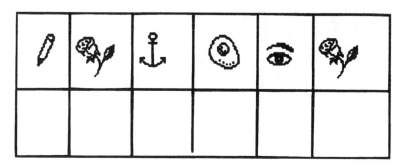

 Is an Outlet    Is a Yolk

 ## Family Project

SHARE YOUR MEMORY VERSE

Review your memory verse (Psalm 6:9) with another Christian this week. Talk together about prayer answers you've each received. Think of new prayer requests to bring before God. Tell your friend that you will be his or her prayer partner, and pray for him or her every day.

Worship God Only

 ## Memory Verse

Matthew 4:10 — *"Thou shalt worship the Lord thy God, and Him only shalt thou serve."* (KJV)

"Worship the Lord your God, and serve Him only." (NIV)

 ## Bible Activity

WHAT IDOLS CAN'T DO

The Israelites bowed before Baal, an idol. God tells what idols are like in Psalm 115:4-7. Draw on the idol the body parts that are named in these verses. Then draw a line from each part to the words which tell what they can't do.

1. CAN'T HANDLE.

2. CAN'T HEAR.

3. CAN'T WALK.

4. CAN'T SMELL.

5. CAN'T SEE.

6. CAN'T SPEAK.

Answer: Lines from 1-hand, 2-ear, 3-foot, 4-nose, 5-eyes, 6-mouth

 ## Family Project

MAKE A PUZZLE

With a pencil copy the memory verse on a piece of cardboard. Have an adult help you cut the cardboard into several pieces to make a puzzle. (If a box cutter is used, a teen brother or dad should use it.) Reassemble the puzzle to review your memory verse.

Bible Activities for Class and Home, Grades 1 and 2

Do Not Fear

 ## Memory Verse

Psalm 118:6 — *"The Lord is on my side; I will not fear: what can man do unto me?"* (KJV)

"The Lord is with me; I will not be afraid. What can man do to me?" (NIV)

 ## Bible Activity

FOLLOW THE DOTS

Follow the dots with your pencil and see what Charles is daring to do even though others may laugh at him.

Answer: He is daring to pray before eating lunch.

 ## Family Project

DISCUSS YOUR FEARS

Do you have any fears? Don't be ashamed. Everyone — even grownups — are sometimes afraid. Perhaps you become afraid when the light is turned out at bedtime. Maybe you're frightened that something bad will happen to a parent. Why not discuss these and other fears with your parents. It usually helps when we share our fears.

He Is My Strength

 Memory Verse

Philippians 4:13 — *"I can do all things through Christ which strengtheneth me."* (KJV)

"I can do everything through Him Who gives me strength." (NIV)

 Bible Activity

POWERFUL STUFF

There are many different kinds of power. Match each picture on the left to its source of power on the right. Draw lines to connect each.

Where can we learn about God's power?

In the _____

Answers: Match people-groceries, sailboat-wind, light bulb-electricity, car-gasoline. Fill in the blanks with BIBLE.

 Family Project

MAKE A SCROLL

Fold a piece of typing paper in half, length-wise. Wrap each short end around a pencil or drinking straw and glue it. On your scroll, print "I CAN DO EVERYTHING THROUGH HIM WHO GIVES ME STRENGTH." Decorate the edges. Roll up your scroll and tie it with a ribbon.

Tell the Truth

 ## Memory Verse

Ephesians 4:25 — *"Putting away lying, speak every man truth with his neighbour."* (KJV)

"Each of you must put off falsehood and speak truthfully to his neighbor." (NIV)

 ## Bible Activity

WHAT PETER FORGOT

Shade every space with a dot in it to find what Peter forgot that you should never forget. What is it?

Answer: TRUTH

 ## Family Project

A REMINDER FOR YOUR ROOM

Have an adult cut four 3 x 10-inch strips from a cardboard box. Print "ALWAYS" on the unprinted side of the first strip. Print "TELL" on the second strip, "THE" on the third, and "TRUTH" on the last. Attach the strips by punching a hole in each end and threading yarn through them. Hang the visual in your room.

The Lord's Supper

 Memory Verse

I Corinthians 11:26 — *"As often as ye eat this bread, and drink this cup, ye do show the Lord's death till He come."* (KJV)

"Whenever you eat this bread and drink this cup, you proclaim the Lord's death until He comes." (NIV)

 Bible Activity

CODED MESSAGE

Draw lines from the numbered dots from 1 to 15, and connect the broken lines on the objects in the middle of the picture.

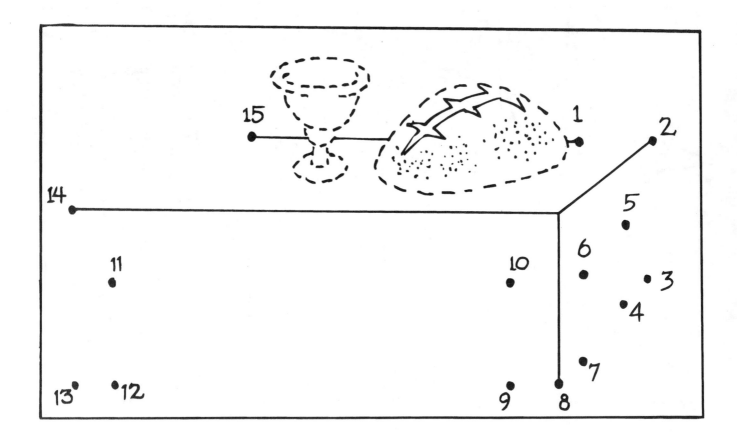

 Family Project

MAKE A PUZZLE

Let's have some fun with the dot-to-dot picture above. Cut out the picture and glue it to a piece of cardboard. Have an adult cut the picture into puzzle pieces. Give the puzzle to a friend and after he or she puts it together, tell your friend about the Bible story pictured.

Give Yourself to God

 Memory Verse

Romans 12:1 — *"Present your bodies a living sacrifice, holy, acceptable unto God."* (KJV)

"Offer your bodies as living sacrifices, holy and pleasing to God." (NIV)

 Bible Activity

IS IT GOOD?

The following pictures show hands, feet, eyes, and ears doing good things or bad things. Circle the number of each picture showing body parts that are doing good. Cross out the number of each picture showing body parts that are not doing good.

Answer: Circle 1, 5, 6; Cross out 2, 3, 4.

 Family Project

MAKE A DOOR HANGER

With your parent's help, cut a 7 x 10-inch sheet from a file folder, construction paper, or poster board. Cut a 2-1/2-inch circle at one end (to fit a door knob). Beneath the circle, print "I GIVE MYSELF TO JESUS." Next draw a picture of yourself under the words. Color your door hanger. Then hang it on your bedroom door knob.

Obey Your Parents

 Memory Verse

Ephesians 6:1 — *"Children, obey your parents in the Lord: for this is right."* (KJV & NIV)

 Bible Activity

MY PROMISE CHART

As you color the frame around your chart, think of ways you can obey your parents this week so your home can be a happy place. Cut out the chart and give it to your mom or dad.

MY PROMISE CHART

Dear _____,

    I promise to obey you. Please color the circle by each day of the week that I obey you. I want our home to be a happy place.

○ SUNDAY   ○ THURSDAY
○ MONDAY   ○ FRIDAY
○ TUESDAY   ○ SATURDAY
○ WEDNESDAY

I love you. _____

 Family Project

FOLLOW YOUR PROMISE CHART

    You know lots of ways to help make your home a happy place. One way is to obey your parents. Give your mom or dad the "Promise Chart" you made above. Give each parent a hug and say, "I love you." Think of two more things you can do this week to make your home happy — and do them!

Bible Activities for Class and Home, Grades 1 and 2

Obey God

 ## Memory Verse

Deuteronomy 33:27 — *"The eternal God is thy refuge, and underneath are the everlasting arms."* (KJV)

"The eternal God is your refuge, and underneath are the everlasting arms." (NIV)

 ## Bible Activity

HOW TO PUT GOD FIRST

How can you put God first? Color each space with a dot in it.

What message do you discover?_____

Do you do what this message says?_____

Answer: Obey God

 ## Family Project

MAKE A PLATE FOR YOUR WALL

With a magic marker, print "GOD IS MY REFUGE" on a paper plate. Have a parent glue around the edge of the plate. Press macaroni into the glue to form a macaroni border. Using crayons, decorate the center of the plate with flowers. Staple yarn on the back and hang the plate on your wall.

Tell Your Friends

 Memory Verse

Matthew 28:19-20 — *"Go ye therefore, and teach all nations...Teaching them to observe all things whatsoever I have commanded you."* (KJV)

"Therefore go and make disciples of all nations...teaching them to obey everything I have commanded you." (NIV)

 Bible Activity

GO AND TELL

Help the children find the way to go and tell the Good News about Jesus. After drawing a path that doesn't cross any lines in the maze, think of one person you can tell about Jesus. Ask God to help you be a good witness.

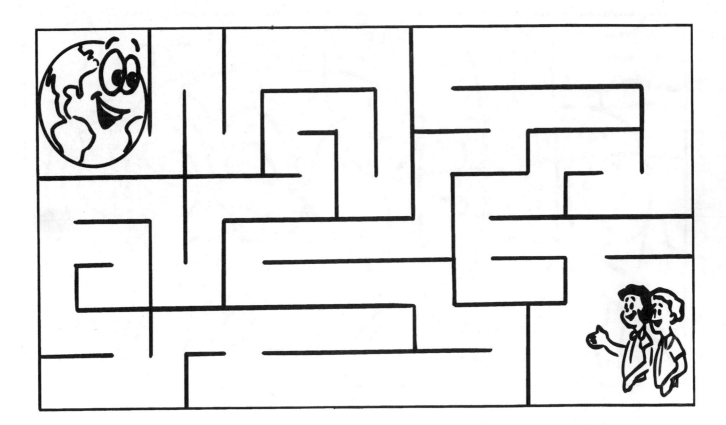

 Family Project

MAKE A SPECIAL OFFERING BANK

Draw and cut out a paper cross and glue it to a margarine cup lid. Ask an adult to cut a 2" slot at the bottom of the cross. Cut out and glue paper hearts for a border around the cross. Put the lid on the cup, making a special offering bank. Save coins to give to a mission offering.

Change for Jesus

 ## Memory Verse

Romans 15:4 — *"Whatsoever things were written aforetime were written for our learning."* (KJV)

"Everything that was written in the past was written to teach us." (NIV)

 ## Bible Activity

WHAT CAN CHANGE YOU?
Cut out the four puzzle pieces and put them together to form a picture that will help you remember your memory verse.

 ## Family Project

MAKE A BOOKMARK

Do you know one Book you can always depend on? Let's make a bookmark for that Book, the Bible. Cut out a 10-inch strip of wide ribbon. Make a picture of Jesus with the words "JESUS FIRST" below it. Cut out the picture and words and glue them to the top of the ribbon. Use the bookmark to mark Bible verses in your Bible.

Part of the Body

 ## Memory Verse

I Corinthians 12:27 — *"Now ye are the body of Christ, and members in particular."* (KJV)

"Now you are the body of Christ, and each one of you is a part of it." (NIV)

 ## Bible Activity

MATCH THE PICTURES

Match the picture of each person with the job that he or she needs to do at church. Draw lines to connect the jobs with people who need to do the jobs.

1.

 (A)

2.

 (B)

3.

 (C)

Answers: 1-B, 2-C, 3-A

 ## Family Project

MAKE A POSTER

Ask your mom or dad to help you make a poster called "PEOPLE SERVING IN MY CHURCH." On a poster board or blank cardboard, paste photos (taken with an instant camera) or print names of people who have special jobs to do at your church. Be sure to include yourself!

Serve the Lord

 Memory Verse

Joshua 24:15 — *"As for me and my house, we will serve the LORD."* (KJV)

"As for me and my household, we will serve the LORD." (NIV)

 Bible Activity

CRACK THE CODE

To discover two things every family needs, look at the picture in each window of the apartment house. Write the first letter of that picture in the space under it.

Answers: LOVE, BIBLE

 Family Project

MAKE LOVE-COUPONS

Cut out some heart-shaped pieces of paper. Write "GOOD FOR ONE HUG" on each one. Give these love-coupons to all the members of your family. When they are given back to you, do what the coupon says to each person who gives the coupon back to you.

Work for the Lord

 ## Memory Verse

I Corinthians 15:58 — *"Always abounding in the work of the Lord...your labor is not in vain in the Lord."* (KJV)

"Always give yourselves fully to the work of the Lord...your labor in the Lord is not in vain." (NIV)

 ## Bible Activity

HELP GOD'S WORKER MAZE

Jim wants to tell Matt how to receive Jesus as his Savior. Satan tries to stop him by giving him excuses. Find a way for Jim to reach Matt. Remember, what you do for Jesus is never in vain.

 ## Family Project

MAKE A JOB LIST

Make a list of special jobs that you feel God wants you to do. For an example, a list might have: Be nice to my sister; Tell Mom I love her; Pick up my toys; Invite a friend to church. Cut the list into pieces, so that each piece has one job on it. Put the slips of paper into a small box. Take out one slip each day and do whatever it says.

Careful Eyes

 ## Memory Verse

Psalm 119:37 — *"Turn away mine eyes from beholding vanity; and quicken Thou me in Thy way."* (KJV)

"Turn my eyes away from worthless things; preserve my life according to Your Word." (NIV)

 ## Bible Activity

LOOKING GOOD!
Draw a line connecting each of the eyes on the left to something good to look at on the right.

Draw lines to the rainbow, church, Bible, and flowers.

 ## Family Project

SCHEDULE YOUR TV

We should be very careful what we watch on TV. Sit down with your family and look at the TV schedule for the week. Decide together what shows would be good for you to see. Circle the shows you decide to watch. Keep the list near the TV. Make sure you don't watch a show that is not circled!

Give to Others

 ## Memory Verse

Matthew 25:35, 40 — *"I was an hungered, and ye gave Me meat.... Inasmuch as ye have done it unto...My brethren, ye have done it unto Me."* (KJV)

"I was hungry and you gave Me something to eat....Whatever you did for...these brothers of Mine, you did for Me." (NIV)

 ## Bible Activity

MIXED UP CHICKENS

Each chick has a letter or number on it. Write this in the square beside the chick's number. Then look up the verse and read it. Color the chicks.

Answer: Matthew 25:40

 ## Family Project

MAKE A GOODY BASKET

Ask your parents for an empty egg carton. Fill each of the compartments with goodies (suggestions: raisins, nuts, marshmallows, etc.). Invite a friend over for a party and share some of your goodies with her.

Read God's Word

 ## Memory Verse

Hebrews 4:12 — *"The Word of God is quick, and powerful, and sharper than any twoedged sword."* (KJV)

"The Word of God is living and active. Sharper than any double-edged sword." (NIV)

 ## Bible Activity

GOD'S WORD SPEAKS TO ME

Color the picture. Glue this page to a piece of cardboard. Cut on the lines to make a jigsaw puzzle. Put the puzzle together, then take it apart. Ask a family member to assemble the puzzle.

 ## Family Project

MAKE A SWORD

Draw a simple sword on an old manila folder. Color your sword and cut it out. Then with a magic marker, print "THE BIBLE SPEAKS TO ME!" on the sword. Tape the sword to your mirror. Every time you look in the mirror, remember that the Bible speaks to you.

Forgive Others

 Memory Verse

Luke 17:3 — *"If thy brother trespass against thee, rebuke him; and if he repent, forgive him."* (KJV)

"If your brother sins, rebuke him, and if he repents, forgive him." (NIV)

 Bible Activity

A FAIR FRIEND
Color the spaces that have a star in them to discover the name of the man who treated his friends fairly when they were unfair to him.

Answer: DAVID

 Family Project

BAKE SOME COOKIES

Can you think of someone who is hard to love? How many ways can you think of to show that person that you love him or her? Ask your mother to help you bake some cookies to put on a paper plate, cover them with plastic wrap, and give them to that person.

Fishers of Men

 ## Memory Verse

Matthew 4:19 — *"Follow Me, and I will make you fishers of men."* (KJV & NIV)

 ## Bible Activity

FISHING REMINDERS

To help you to remember to be "fishers of men," color and cut out the fish. Write the name of someone you can witness to on each fish. Place the fish on your dresser or desk. After witnessing to each person, glue the "fish" to a poster to hang on your wall.

 ## Family Project

MAKE A WALKING FISH

From colored paper cut out a fish (using one of the fish above for a pattern) and draw and cut out four small footprints. Print on the fish, "FOLLOW JESUS AND FISH FOR MEN." Tape strings to the footprints and the fish and tie a string loop at the top for hanging.

Learn God's Ways

 Memory Verse

Psalm 119:73 — *"Thy hands have made me and fashioned me: give me understanding, that I may learn Thy commandments."* (KJV)

"Your hands made me and formed me; give me understanding to learn Your commands." (NIV)

 Bible Activity

DAVID GREW UP RIGHT

David used a stone to kill an enemy giant. Each stone has a number or letter on it. Write this in the space beside each stone's number. Then look up the verse and read it. Color the stones different colors.

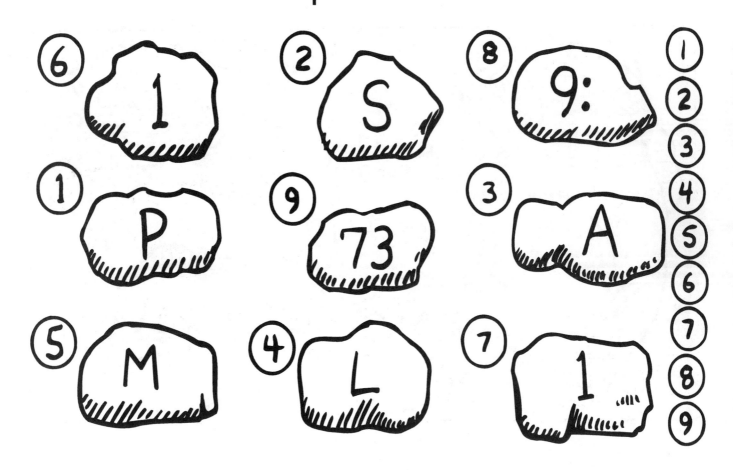

 Family Project

MAKE A HEIGHT CHART

Cut three sheets of construction paper in half, lengthwise. Glue the ends together to make one long strip. Print the memory verse (Psalm 119:73) starting one foot from the top of the strip. Tape your chart to the wall to measure your growth. Make a mark on the chart to show your height today. Print today's date next to the mark.

Be a Good Witness

 ## Memory Verse

John 13:35 — *"By this shall all men know that ye are My disciples, if ye have love one to another."* (KJV)

"All men will know that you are My disciples, if you love one another." (NIV)

 ## Bible Activity

HIDDEN PICTURE

Sharing helps you to be a living witness. Hidden in the picture are some things you can share. There are twelve things to find. Can you find all twelve?

Answers: Bible; football; ice cream cone; baseball; car; doll; cupcake; skateboard; scooter; wagon; baseball bat; smile

 ## Family Project

MAKE A WALL CRAFT

Color the edges of three small (dessert-dish size) paper plates. Draw and color a red heart in the center of the first. On the second, print, "SHOW YOUR LOVE BY." On the third, print, "HOW YOU LIVE." Glue the plates to a ribbon. Hang the craft on your bedroom wall.

Do Your Best

 ## Memory Verse

Psalm 18:32 — *"It is God that girdeth me with this strength, and maketh my way perfect."* (KJV)

"It is God who arms me with strength and makes my way perfect." (NIV)

 ## Bible Activity

DOING-MY-BEST CHART

For one week keep a record of doing your best for each activity indicated on the chart below. Put a check mark each day you tried to do your best. (Today will be Day 1, tomorrow, Day 2, etc.) When the chart is filled, show it to your parents.

ACTIVITY	DAYS OF THE WEEK						
	1	2	3	4	5	6	7
MADE MY BED							
CLEANED MY ROOM							
READ MY BIBLE							
PRAYED							
LEARNED A BIBLE VERSE							
EXERCISED							

 ## Family Project

LEARNING FROM YOUR PARENTS

Ask your parents to help you learn to do one thing better — Like riding a bike, pitching a ball, reading, swimming, or anything else. Add that to your chart above and work hard to do your best learning it this week. Remember to ask God to help you do your best.

Bible Activities for Class and Home, Grades 1 and 2

Be a Good Friend

 Memory Verse

Romans 13:8 — *"Love one another: for he that loveth another hath fulfilled the law."* (KJV)

"Love one another, for he who loves his fellowman has fulfilled the law." (NIV)

 Bible Activity

ARE YOU A GOOD FRIEND?

David and Jonathan were good friends. Circle the children who are being good friends. Color those pictures.

Answers: Circle and color children in 3 & 4.

 Family Project

VISIT SOME OLDER PERSONS

Be a good friend to some older persons. With your parents visit grandparents, shut-ins, or a nursing home. Sing songs, say some Bible verses, talk to them, and give them fruit or cookies. Perhaps you and some other children can make this visit together.

Cheer Up Your Friends

 ## Memory Verse

Proverbs 17:17 — *"A friend loveth at all times, and a brother is born for adversity."* (KJV)

"A friend loves at all times, and a brother is born for adversity." (NIV)

 ## Bible Activity

A FRIENDLY NOTE

Cut out the note below and glue it on a large 4 x 6-inch index card. Color it with bright colors. Print the name and address of a friend on the other side of the card and add a stamp. Mail the card to cheer up your friend.

I'M GLAD WE'RE FRIENDS!

 ## Family Project

A CARD FOR A FAR-AWAY FRIEND

We all like to get letters from our friends? Think of a friend or relative that lives far away that you don't see very often. Send them a letter or postcard this week. If you have a picture of yourself or your family, send it along.

Show Your Love

Memory Verse

I Thessalonians 3:12 — *"The Lord make you to increase...in love one toward another, and toward all men."* (KJV)

"The Lord make your love increase...for each other and for everyone else." (NIV)

Bible Activity

THE GARDEN OF LOVE

Think of someone who needs your love. Write their names under the rock that names a specific way you can show love to a person.

sharing

kind words

hugs

smiling

say, "I love you"

helping

Family Project

DECORATE COOKIES

Spread cream cheese on sugar cookies. Decorate the cookies with pieces of fruit. Mandarin oranges and maraschino cherries work well! Now serve the cookies to your family. Let others choose first. Try to decorate the cookies so they are all equally nice.

Be Cheerful

Memory Verse

Proverbs 17:22 — *"A merry heart doeth good like a medicine: but a broken spirit drieth the bones."* (KJV)

"A cheerful heart is good medicine, but a crushed spirit dries up the bones." (NIV)

Bible Activity

OUR ACTIONS SPEAK

Some of the children below are smiling. But others are frowning. Color only the children who are smiling. Their smiles speak of love for God. How many children did you color? _____ How many children are frowning?_____ Circle the face below that shows how you might feel right now.

Answers: Color four smiling children. Three are frowning.

Family Project

SHOW YOUR PARENTS LOVE

Tell your parents that you love them. But don't just leave it at that. Tell them you want to show that you love them by doing something nice for them. Ask them to assign you a household chore. Perform it cheerfully and with care. This is an opportunity to prove that your actions match your words.